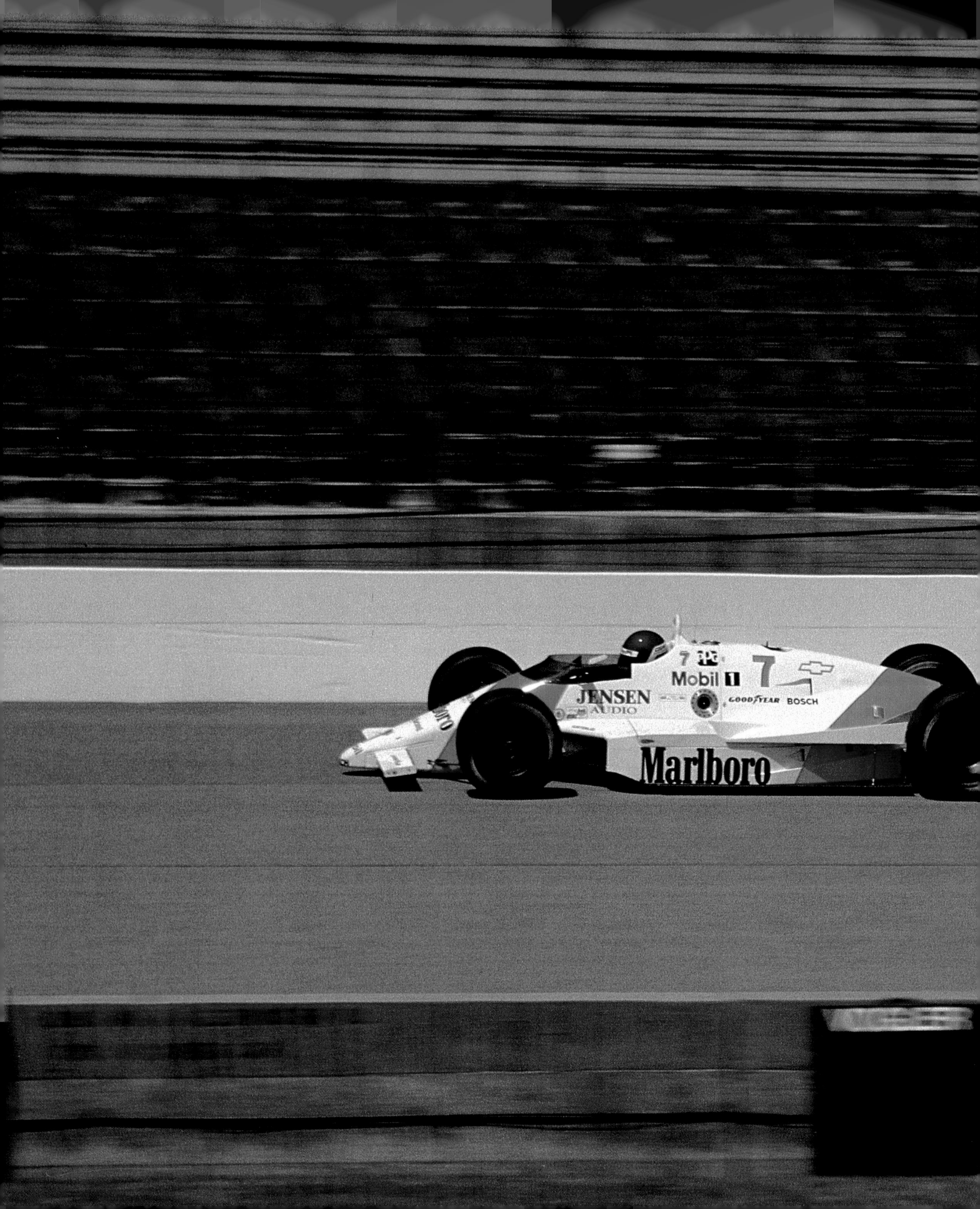

Mobil 1
JENSEN AUDIO
GOODYEAR
BOSCH
Marlboro

INDY RACE CARS

From behind the garage doors

*The month of May
at Indianapolis*

Dave Arnold

Motorbooks International
Publishers & Wholesalers Inc
Osceola, Wisconsin 54020, USA ®

To Martha Jean, my wife, the mother of our children and my best friend

First published in 1989 by Motorbooks International Publishers & Wholesalers Inc, P O Box 2, 729 Prospect Avenue, Osceola, WI 54020 USA

© Dave Arnold, 1989

Printed and bound in Hong Kong

The information in this book is true and complete to the best of our knowledge. All recommendations are made without any guarantee on the part of the author or publisher, who also disclaim any liability incurred in connection with the use of this data or specific details

We recognize that some words, model names and designations, for example, mentioned herein are the property of the trademark holder. We use them for identification purposes only. This is not an official publication

Library of Congress Cataloging-in-Publication Data
Arnold, Dave
  Indy Race Cars: From behind the garage doors.

  1. Indianapolis Speedway Race. I. Title.
GV1033.5.I55A76 1989   796.7'2'0977252
ISBN 0-87938-335-6   88-13730

Motorbooks International books are also available at discounts in bulk quantity for industrial or sales-promotional use. For details write to Special Sales Manager at the Publisher's address

On the front cover: *The Granatelli Indy car at speed.*

Inset: *A mechanic works on the rear end of an Indy race car.*

On the back cover: *A. J. Foyt makes an inspection of the running of a Cosworth engine.*

On the frontispiece: *The smooth bodywork of a Chevrolet-Marlboro car.*

On the title page: *Time trials for the Chevrolet-engined car. Tim Parker*

On the contents page: *The Borg-Warner trophy, symbolic of first place at Indy, was first awarded in 1936. Since that race it annually receives the head bust of the most recent winner. In spite of its obvious rarity and value (it's made of pure sterling silver), it nevertheless is on public display in the pits every day of practice and qualifying during May.*

BO

Contents

Gasoline Alley
In the paddock

The month of May at Indy is like no other period in racing anywhere around the world. Virtually thirty full days are devoted to readying a race car for a single race. On-site preparation for the Michigan 500, for example, is a three- to five-day affair before the one day of racing. Many other events on the Indy car circuit, usually those with shorter tracks and smaller crowds, will only see cars and teams appear on a Friday, with Saturday being a day for preparation and Sunday being qualification and race day. By Sunday evening the track will be empty of transporters and crews until the nomadic teams make their next visit.

Indianapolis, however, becomes an encampment, a home away from home for the entire month. Qualifications are not limited to an hour or two immediately before race time; rather, they occupy two entire weekends before the race is held. Moreover, qualification spectators at Indianapolis aren't just those who arrive well ahead of the race, as is the case at most tracks. Qualifications at Indianapolis are a major event in themselves, attracting literally hundreds of thousands of spectators to see who earns the pole position. In fact, qualifications alone at Indianapolis generate far larger crowds and far more publicity than do actual racing events in other parts of the world.

Obviously there are reasons for all this, and they pretty much boil down to money and fame. The Indianapolis 500 race, dating from 1911, was conceived initially to be a very large, heavily publicized, single annual event to be held at the Brickyard. Big prize money, big names from the racing and entertainment worlds and worldwide

Airy, well lighted, clean and simply constructed of nonflamable materials (primarily masonry products), these garages become the home away from home for crews during the month of May. Teams may make modifications to their quarters; here the Penske team has tiled the floor with the traditional black-and-white checkered-flag look of winners. There are a total of 96 individual garages for race cars in the Alley, and large teams will rent adjoining units with folding walls that can be collapsed, resulting in one large room. Tim Parker

publicity were envisioned from the beginning.

Add to this the fact that America was just beginning its love affair with the automobile, and it's not hard to see that the founders had developed a winning formula which has not been altered to this day.

Prize money in 1988 totaled over $5.1 million, with the winner receiving the lion's share of $804,000. The thirty-third and last-place finisher in 1988 came very close to receiving $100,000. In other words, just making the starting field at Indianapolis virtually guarantees $100,000. As for the crowds? How does the world's largest single-day sporting event sound? Well over 400,000 people cram into the infield and stands surrounding the 2½ mile oval, and millions more watch TV coverage. Attendance during the two qualification weekends combined nearly double the on-site race day attendance. So the formula established in 1911 still works in 1988.

Just what goes on at Indianapolis for thirty or more days? Why do teams actually spend that much time living away from home and incurring staggering expenses? And, is it really necessary to devote this much time and effort to a single race? Simply put, the answer seems to be yes to all three questions, and the reasons all seem to relate to the "ten-tenths" nature of the event. That is, if you're going to spend the money to participate in the first place, and if you want a good chance of doing well and perhaps even winning, then you and your team are going to have to do what everyone else does—work for perfection in all aspects of your car's and your team's performance. In other words, it's competition for your share of over $5 million of prize money and the worldwide publicity and credibility that go with a good performance. Competition at the ten-tenths level virtually forces you to spend thirty days searching for the perfect combination of variables that will bring success.

A look at a typical portion of the garages in the Alley. Rebuilt in 1986 using fire-resistant materials, a hot May sun makes the Alley seem more like an adobe village in the southwestern United States than a racing facility in the Midwest. Entering a single car in the 500 with all associated fees, licenses and garage rental costs a team about $7,400. Since many teams rent a block of three to five garages and enter as many cars, the costs quickly skyrocket to the $30,000 range just to be present, let alone turn a wheel on the track.

What is it like for the driver and crew for those thirty days? Well, it depends on how the car is performing. If you're fast right out of the box and you don't break or damage too much equipment, the pace can seem rational, maybe even fun. But if the car runs slow, especially if you thought it would be fast, the next thirty days can become an agony of nonstop efforts to find the combination necessary to make the car perform. Tension and frustration result. Long working hours become *very* long working hours. Interruptions become unbearable and the possibility of a crash requiring extensive rebuilding becomes unthinkable—until it happens. In the background is the ever-present media reporting each team's activities and compiling daily reports for wide-ranging distribution. The scent of $100 cologne, and $500 business suits, become more common as the month wears on; the sponsors are in town, just to see how things are going. They sure would like to see their name up with the front-runners. Corporate logos on a front-row car receive a lot more exposure than those on a back marker.

Experienced crews that have been through Indy's Thirty Days of May are able to take much of this in stride. They come back to Indy each year knowing the unexpected is the rule, and they recognize that worrying about a car's performance won't make it perform better. They seem to differ little from top athletes before a major athletic contest—they're able to put the bright lights, publicity and dollars behind them and focus on the task at hand. Distractions and mechanical problems don't seem to deter them from the course they have set for themselves.

So, keeping in mind that Indy is a ten-tenths activity worth millions in terms of publicity and actual dollars, let's take a look at Gasoline Alley and see what goes on behind the scenes.

The Buick office in Gasoline Alley with a ready supply of V-6 stock-block powerplants. With Cosworth engines at about $60,000 dollars and the turbocharged Chevrolet V-8 at over $80,000, the Buick seems like a good deal at around $45,000. It gets even better though, when you realize that Buick in fact didn't even sell their engines at Indy—they were on loan from the Division. The bottom line is that Buick incurred and absorbed the cost of each engine as a marketing and public relations expense. Those teams with whom Buick reached an agreement and who were willing to modify chassis in order to accommodate the engine were given free use of the powerplants!

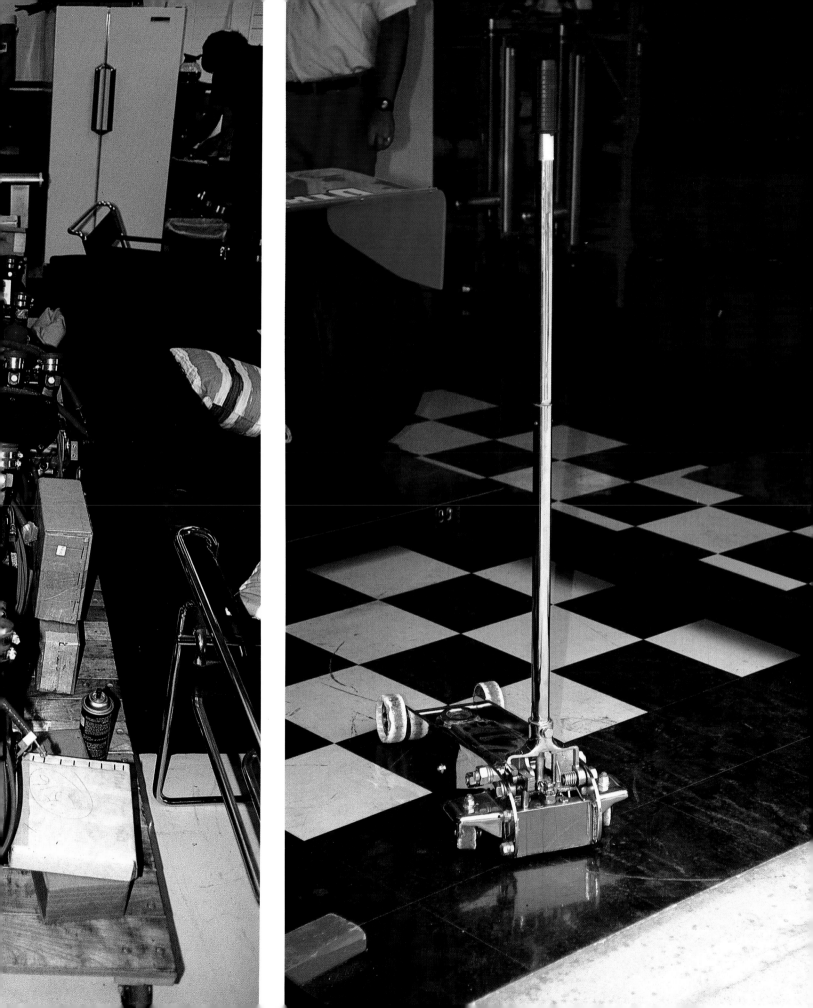

Previous page

While chroming an ordinary jack obviously isn't necessary, it does illustrate the overall concern for quality and cleanliness found throughout the Alley. Tiled floors, organized tools, clean uniforms, daily washing of garage areas and constant polishing all exemplify a serious concern that a sponsor's car and facility look first class in the public eye, and that every attempt is being made to ensure the car will operate in the same manner.

Not every team at Indy is as organized and efficient as the Penske outfit. Long work hours, mechanical problems, just plain bad luck and fatigue all contribute to a team garage which could use a good straightening. Compared to sprint car racing and the conditions found in the work areas at many other tracks, however, this scene is heaven to many mechanics and crew chiefs.

Will the real Bobby Rahal please blink. In addition to the mega-dollar transporters found in the parking areas, the more affluent teams also bring in large, expensive motorhomes, equipped with gourmet chefs and elaborate cooking facilities. Large sun-shielding canopies cover lawn furniture, wet bars and buffet food lines serving teams, drivers and personnel from sponsoring organizations. Indy's high profile results in many visitors who have business connections to the race; thus the need to see that they are properly taken care of during the time trials and race. Tim Parker

Johnny Parsons, Jr., son of a famous Indy driver from the 1950s, operates on his helmet in pit lane prior to a practice run. Vision is a constant problem in an open cockpit car in virtually all types of racing including the 500. Oil, coolant fluids and grime all collect on a transparent face mask and impair a driver's view of the track and competitors—not a happy situation when traveling 200 mph in close traffic. In this particular shot Parsons is applying tape over the upper portion of the face shield to block out sun on a bright May day.

Lest you mistakenly think all the big dollars are inside the confines of Gasoline Alley at Indianapolis, take a look at the transporter parking area. Megabuck haulers abound, complete with fully furnished machine shops and repair facilities. The latest in aerodynamic over-the-road shapes, plush tractor interiors and sleeper cabs predominate. The Penske team came to Indianapolis in 1988 with three trucks: a so-called Race Truck, a Test Truck and a Fuel Truck. The Race Truck, with a digital automatic transmission, can carry three race cars,

spare parts and tools, and is outfitted with generators, compressors and related equipment. Empty of race cars, its value is pegged at $250,000. With three race cars inside, just over $1 million hits the road. The Test Truck can carry 68,000-72,000 pounds and is crammed full of testing devices and equipment. It can carry two race cars and is used to travel to tracks for private testing sessions. The Fuel Truck can carry 550 gallons of fuel along with golf carts, fuel tanks and hoses, nitrogen bottles, air guns and so on.

Back in the pits and hanging from the "hook" this car displays signs of having experienced a minor fire problem as evidenced by the white fire extinguisher dust to the rear and right-hand sides of the car. Safety and emergency crews at Indianapolis have exemplary records in dealing with problems. Disabled racers are typically removed from harm's way in the manner shown here. A racer is designed so that its entire weight can be raised by lifting the rollover bar positioned just behind a driver's head. With numerous emergency vehicles positioned around the track, drivers and damaged cars are never more than a few seconds from help and quick removal from a dangerous position.
Tim Parker

Let's see now, which one of the trillion adjustments do we want to try this time to see if it will go faster? There seems to be nothing else on earth that can soak up as many hours of maintenance and adjustment for every hour it spends in operation as a race car. The various combinations of adjustments and their respective effects on performance seem almost endless. Then, just when everything seems right, a weather change, high temperature and high humidity for example, will have a major effect on horsepower and tire adhesion, requiring a crew to start the dialing-in process all over again. Heaven forbid an accident, which could require replacing suspension components or the engine; changing major components often greatly compounds the problem of getting a car up to speed and keeping it there. Tim Parker

19

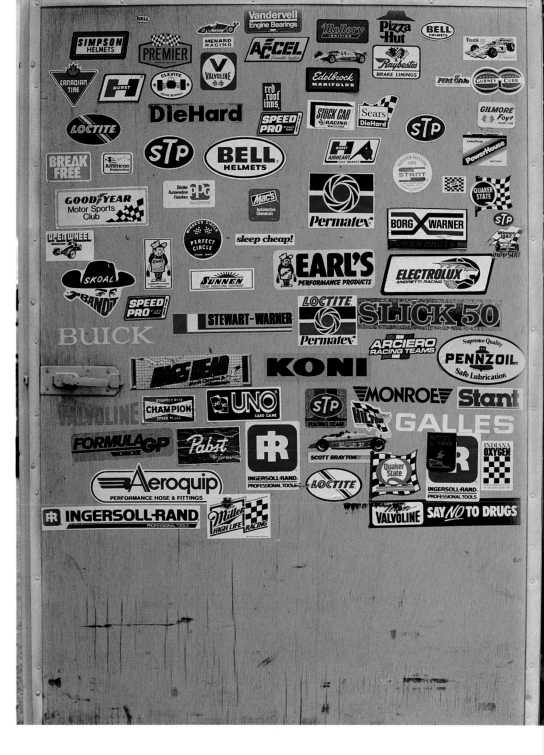

Well-stocked parts bins, metal lathes, hydraulic presses, computerized testing equipment and air conditioning are commonplace in the large mobile repair and rebuilding shops that top teams bring to Indy.

The racing industry is exceeded by few others when it comes to promoting its products, services and even its very existence. Lap prize money, contingency awards, product and service donations, national advertising campaigns and so forth are important elements in the economics of racing. Represented here are many of the sponsors who have become household names in the shops around Gasoline Alley.

Previous page
A view of a typical garage space in Gasoline Alley. The Alley contains 96 16 x 20 foot garages in total, and each garage rents for $1,000 for the month of May.

It's first thing in the morning, by Indianapolis standards at least, and the Granatelli team is just in the early stages of firing and warming a Cosworth for the coming day's activities. Everybody gathers around on an occasion such as this and all cast a critical ear to the first few strokes of life, listening for any possible indications of problems. Starting a cold high-performance racing engine is not a task to be taken lightly, and furrowed brows reflect the concern. The Ilmore

Chevy racing engine is particularly sensitive to cold starts. The Patrick Racing Team, for example, normally will drain all coolant from their Chevy-engined car and refill with boiling coolant to heat up the block. Additionally, a heavy-duty hair dryer is placed under the intake plenum to heat fuel distribution and metering equipment, which is composed of parts with extremely close tolerances and very fine openings.

A sign that something is going right for someone: Roger Penske takes a break to enjoy an ice cream. When things aren't working, everyone is in the garage, rachets twirling, backs bent over the car and no time for a breather. When things are going right, the garages tend to be empty of activity—unless a team decides to tear the whole car apart one last time to see if just a bit more speed can be found somewhere inside.

The cars
Bodywork to cut air

The typical tub of an Indy race car with virtually every major component removed. It is this composite and sandwich constructed unit that is the driver's "office," and to which all other major components, engine suspension, aerodynamic bodywork and so forth are attached. Major structural or misalignment damage to a tub typically requires starting all over, that is, stripping off all usable components, acquiring a new tub and starting the difficult task of dialing in all the various adjustments and combinations before a harmonious and fast car can again be realized. The shiny vertical surface is the equivalent of a firewall in that the engine is mounted directly against it while an oil tank is located on the opposite or cockpit side. The two holes in the black area to the left and slightly below the PPG emblem are mounting holes for the car's engine. Miscellaneous hoses, fuel lines, electrical connections and control cables hang from their respective locations.

The Porsche-engined, March-chassis
Porsche Team car being readied for a
tow to pit lane. The year 1988 was
difficult for the Porsche team in the
United States. Their efforts to compete
in the USAC/CART series met with
much less success than initially hoped
for. Early races proved so
disappointing, the team took the
obviously difficult step of discarding
their own chassis and acquiring a
March unit. Even then, good results
proved elusive, with the car qualifying
for the Indy race in seventeenth
position. For 1988, as in recent years,
the English Cosworth and English Lola
or March chassis or the English-
inspired Penske cars remained the
combinations to beat.

The top rear and lower side pod sections removed from a car undergoing extensive, though typical, maintenance work. These components are constructed from carbon fiber or Kevlar materials, well known for their extreme strength and very light weight. While carbon fiber does not burn, it does lose its strength and rigidity rapidly under high-temperature conditions. Carbon fiber also shatters into many pieces when impacted, while Kevlar will dent or puncture but not shatter.

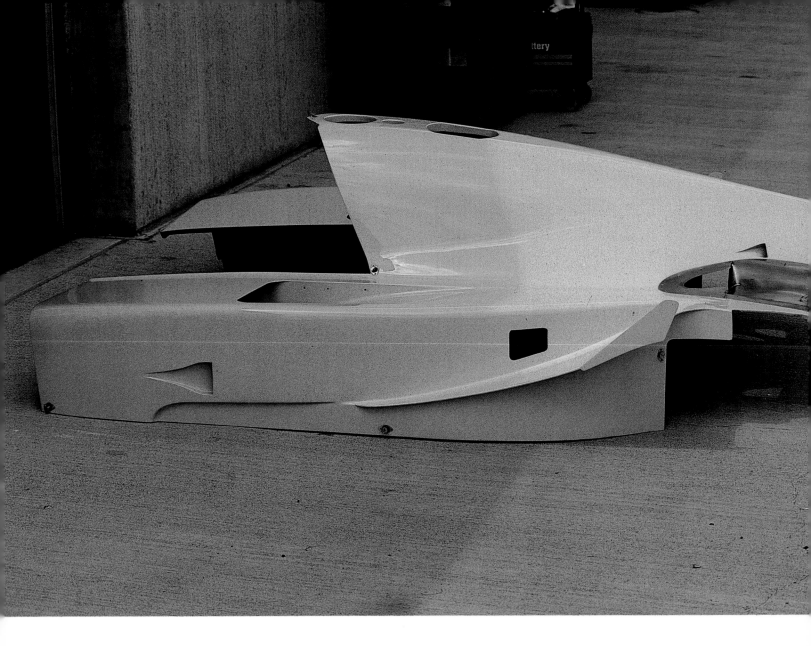

What is the difference between these two rear shrouds for the Penske team's PC-17 cars? Well, the unmarked housing cost the team a few thousand dollars to acquire, while the decorated shroud brings literally hundreds of thousands of sponsorship dollars into the team's coffers. It is generally acknowledged that even the smallest sponsor logo on a typical Indy car will cost a minimum of $50,000 (there are none of these smaller logos to be seen on this Penske shroud). Major sponsors will contribute sums approaching $1 million for a season's racing campaign.

Rear wings on Indy cars tend to be of two types, one being the single-surface, fairly simple affair shown here. A race car wing is nothing more complex than an airplane wing turned upside down; however, contrary to the airplane wing which generates an upward force lifting an aircraft, this wing generates a downward force pushing the race car down. The sideplates are present to force air to flow from front to back over the wing rather than having it spill off the outer edges. They extend primarily below the wing rather than above because controlling flow over the bottom surface is more important and more difficult than controlling flow over the top surface.

35

Previous page
The second type of rear wing is a more complex multi-surfaced piece. Designers seldom agree totally on theories behind their choice of devices, but no doubt it is argued that this larger, more complex wing creates no more drag than its smaller cousin. Regardless of the drag issue, large sideplates are a problem in crosswind conditions.

A rear wing still mounted to the transaxle cover. Note also the transaxle cooler. The mounting of a rear wing must be very well engineered since, in addition to vibration and related stress, the wing will generate approximately 500 to 700 pounds of downforce when an Indy car is traveling at 200 mph. In Indy configuration, aerodynamics will add about 1,500 pounds of downforce to a car at speed. In road course configuration, the same car will be set up so that aerodynamics add approximately 3,500 pounds of downforce.

Previous page
A USAC official checking wing mountings for security and proper design on John Andretti's 1988 Lola Cosworth. Rear wings receive extra-special attention on race cars because of the forces they generate and the effect they have on a car's handling. Failure of any component on a race car is a serious issue, but failure of a rear wing will instantly unload the car's suspension, creating a situation of limited tire adhesion on a vehicle that may be traveling 200 mph in a corner.

The front wing on an Indy car, generating far less force than a rear wing, is used primarily to balance or fine-tune a car's handling characteristics. Drivers and mechanics tend to use the terms "more wing" or "less wing" when referring to adjustments. More wing equates to increasing the pitch or angle of the wing's cord (an imaginary straight line running from the leading edge of the wing to the trailing edge) in relation to the "relative wind" or the air through which the wing is moving. As the wing angle is increased (the trailing edge is raised or the front edge is lowered, or both changes are made simultaneously), it will create more downforce on the car. This downforce increases the traction, in this case to the front of the car, but it also increases aerodynamic drag which will hurt performance at high speed. The real challenge with front and rear wings is to create as much downforce as needed with as little aerodynamic drag as possible—and while accomplishing these twin goals, also being sure to keep the force generated by the wings in balance. Balancing both ends of a race car to achieve maximum cornering capability and minimum high-speed drag is only one of the skills in the black science of preparing an Indy car.

The quick-fill valve in the side of a typical Indy car has done much to speed up pit stops during a race. Its size and construction allow the transfer of 40 gallons of fuel, fed under gravity pressure only, in about 15 seconds. The male fitting on the fuel hose need only be pushed into the valve and held firmly in position by the fueler to allow fuel to flow. At Indianapolis, a race car may not carry more than 40 gallons of fuel while at racing speeds. The methanol fuel is burned at the rate of approximately 1.8 mpg—nearly 1.5 gallons per each 2.5 mile lap.

Gone are the days of exposed engines and exhaust headers. With smaller engines turning a zillion rpm, turbochargers capturing and using cast-off exhaust heat and bundles of exhaust pipes kept inside bodywork for streamlining purposes, the typical Indy race car has a designed-in problem with shedding operational heat. Shown here are heat blisters, along with a developing crack, in the turbocharger area of A. J. Foyt's March chassis, which was running a big-block-based Chevrolet V-6 engine.

The colorful exhaust tail pipe and wastegate pipe exiting a Cosworth engine. Note the closeness of these heat-producing pipes to the car's transaxle and the shielding designed to protect the unit from as much of this heat as possible.

Next page

This close-up of the right side pod on a Lola shows the mechanically driven fuel pump at left, with its associated braided plumbing and flexible drive disappearing toward the engine bay. Ignition and fuel boxes are on the right. The ignition box houses the coil and the electronics which drive the coil and distributor. The fuel box monitors level of turbo boost and adjusts fuel flow to the engine in accordance with predetermined combinations. The radiator just to the right does not create a heat problem for these sensitive devices as it may at first appear. Duct work in the top of the side pod housing immediately behind the radiator exhausts hot air up out of the pod away from the electronics. Additionally, while not clear in this photo, most teams provide a fresh-air duct in the area where the tub meets the side pod, which bathes these devices in cool air.

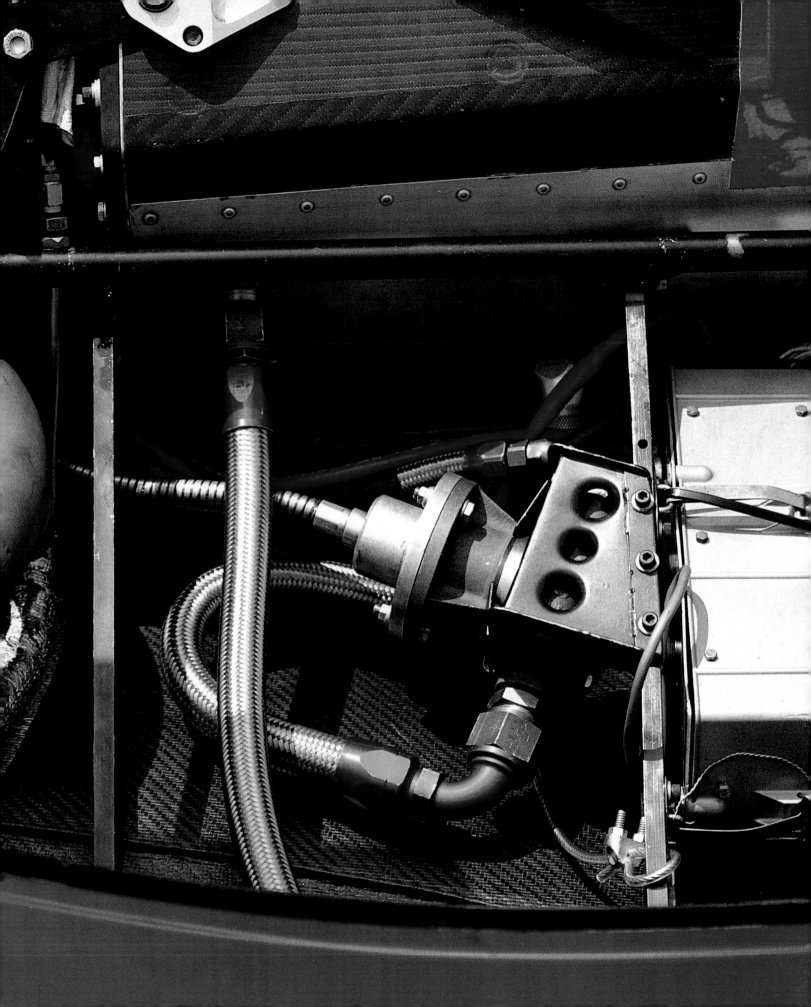

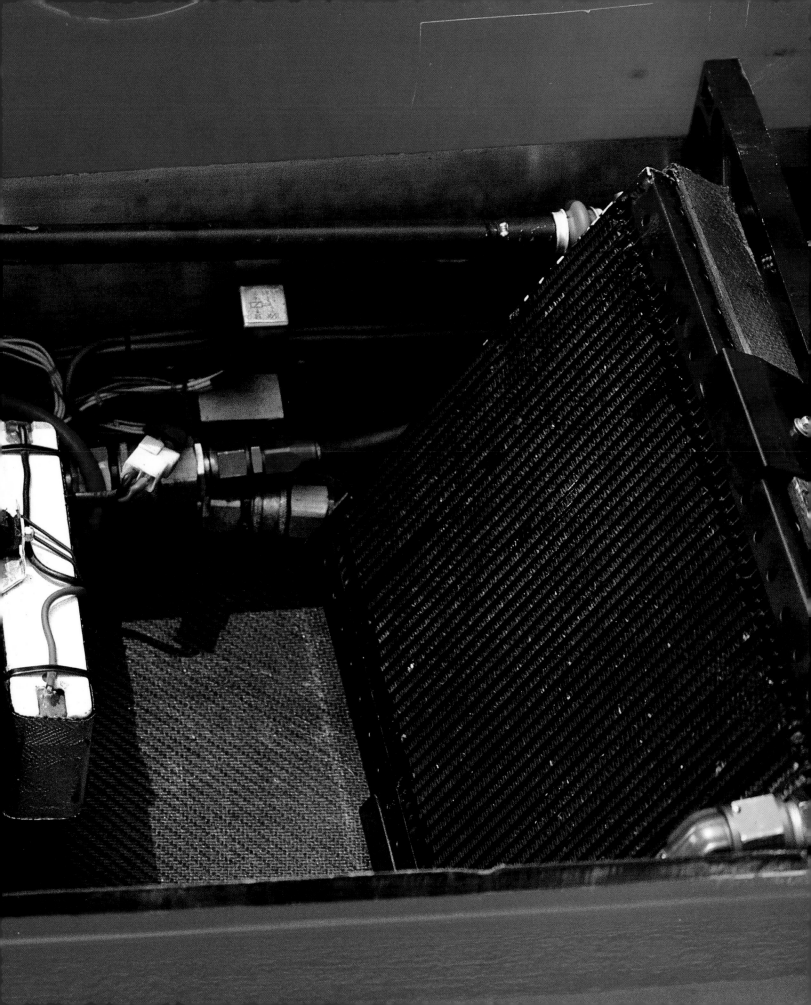

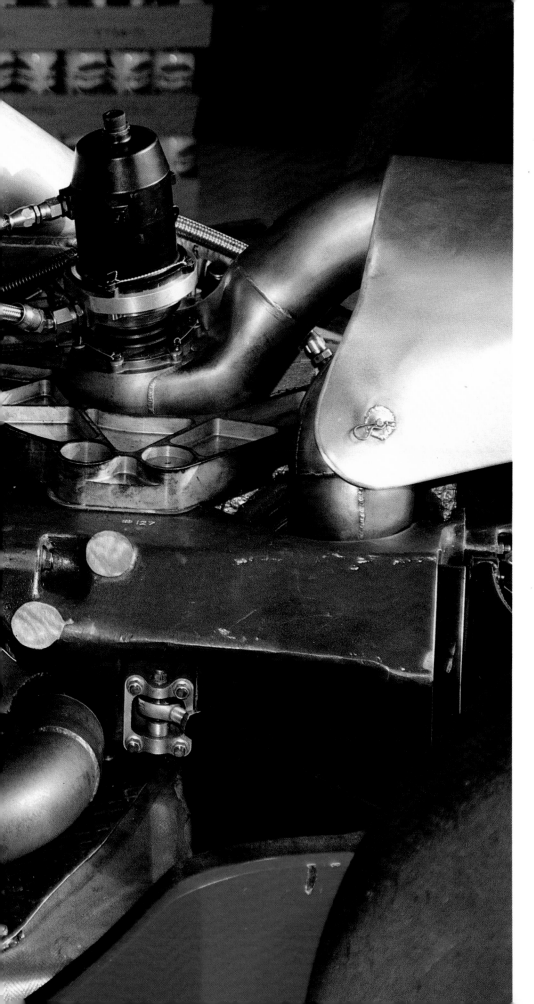

The engines
Stock blocks to turbochargers

The 1988 Judd V-8, in this case
mounted in a 1988 Lola chassis.
Supposedly based on a Honda Formula
One design, in many people's minds it
is a very close cousin (to put it politely)
of the Cosworth V-8.

A stock-block Chevy crankshaft receiving the good old soap-and-water treatment following a complete engine teardown.

Pneumatic wheel lugnut wrenches shine in the sun on pit row awaiting the moment when they will be frantically grabbed by crew members seeking to cut seconds off already too brief pit stops. At racing speeds, one second standing still in the pits equals 300 feet on the track. Failure to quickly loosen or secure wheel lugs can mean many racing car lengths on the track or, even worse, an errant tire and wheel assembly and a resultant three-wheeled race car on the track. Each team's lugnut wrenches must be formally tested by USAC inspection crews to ensure they generate proper torque before they can be used in the pits.

A little maintenance work being performed on a Lola transaxle with the aid of an uncommonly large torque wrench. The nut being tightened required 200 lb-ft of torque, and the length of the wrench gave little doubt the figure easily would be achieved.

Previous page
The all-conquering Cosworth DFX V-8, winner at every 500 from 1978 through 1987. Its brother, the DFZ model, designed with shorter stroke and higher rpm in mind, has been the engine to beat at Indy. These powerplants along with superior chassis from companies like Lola and March have made the English connection the dominant force in racing in the United States and Europe for the past 15 years. The typical Indy Cosworth engine costs approximately $60,000 without turbocharger and exhaust system. It will generate about 390 lb-ft of torque and approach 800 hp in a very high state of tune.

The Penske Chevy Indy V-8 as mounted in a 1988 March chassis. Note the braided steel fuel lines which enter the intake plenum directly above each intake throat. The turbocharged overhead cam Chevrolet V-8, like the Cosworth, Porsche and Judd engines, is allowed a maximum of 161 ci displacement and 45 in. hg manifold pressure, which is barely 7 psi or half an atmosphere of boost pressure.

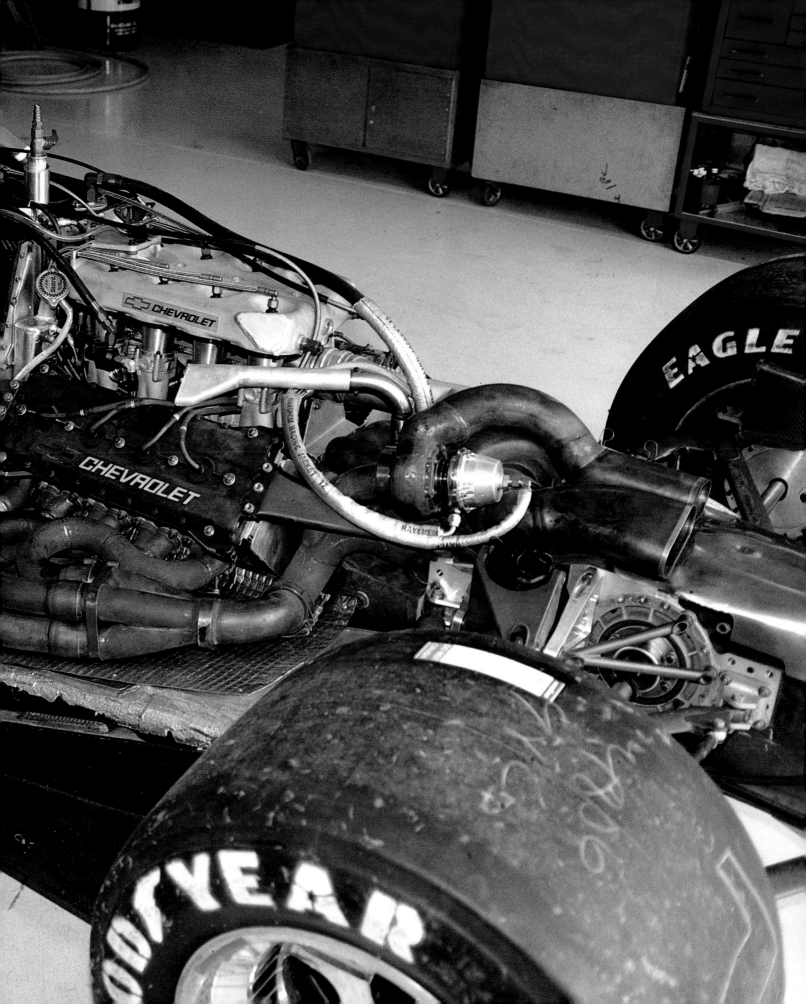

Yes, stock-block Chevrolet V-8s still do show up at Indy. Shown here, in an obviously disassembled state, is a 355 ci naturally-aspirated motor which has just been removed from a March chassis. The Indy limit on a stock-block nonturbocharged engine is actually 390 ci, but this team's 390 had destroyed itself prior to the 355 taking the same route. As mentioned, in addition to other problems facing the Chev stock block, including its lack of serious development by big-dollar teams, it also has a torque problem relative to the Lola and March transaxles. A well-prepared stock-block V-8, in Indy trim, will produce approximately 600 lb-ft of torque while a Cosworth will produce approximately 390 lb-ft. The Lola and March transaxles were never designed to withstand such loads.

A Garrett turbocharger and associated plumbing after removal from Buick V-6 powerplant. This particular unit had developed cracks in the flexible portions of the long pipes extending to the sides and was being replaced with a unit carrying pipes of a different material.

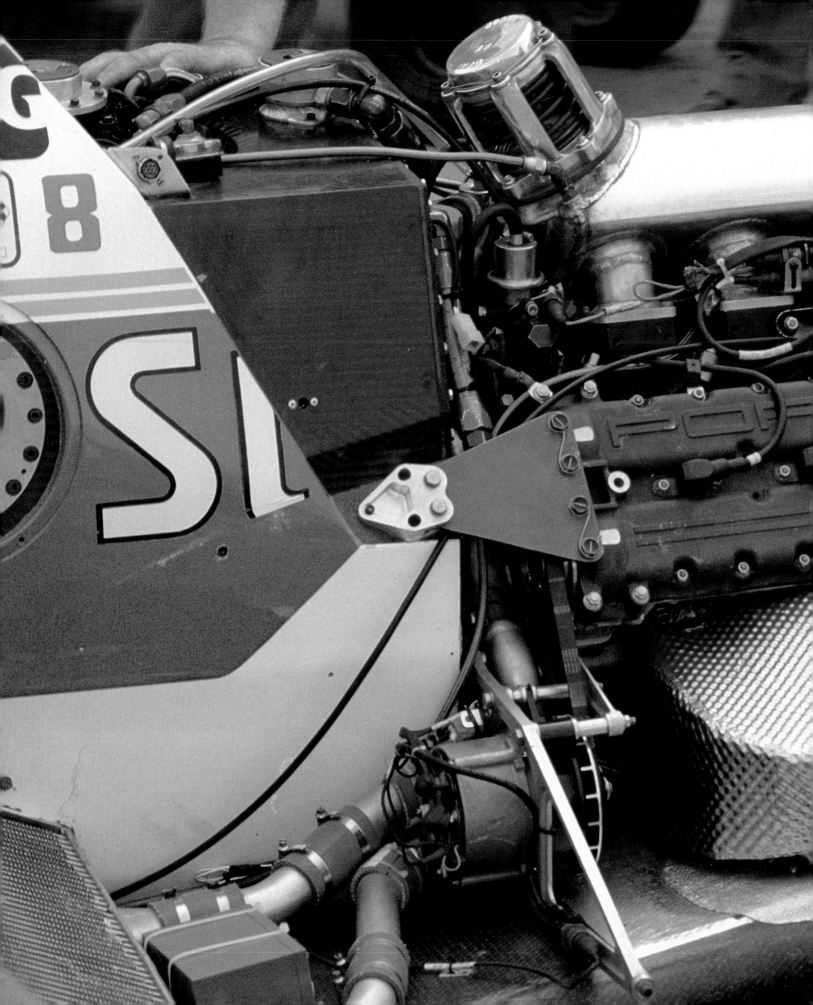

The Indy Porsche V-8, an engine about which little was written during May at Indianapolis. As is obvious from this and other pictures, the days of widely differing engine, chassis, suspension and bodywork designs are gone. It takes a close look to note the difference between a March and Lola chassis, and were it not for nameplates, engines too could be equally difficult to distinguish.

Another engine used in the 500 during recent years is the USAC/CART version of the Honda V-8 Formula One racing engine. Seen here with its lubricating oil being warmed prior to the first start-up for the day, this tremendously successful Grand Prix engine failed to achieve similar results in the United States, primarily due to a lack of overall development effort. Tim Parker

A turbocharged Cosworth V-8 mounted in a 1987 March chassis. Of special note is the silver bare metal box mounted on the aft end of the Cosworth head in line with the upper portion of the camshaft cover. This device, with its long cable which disappears forward toward the driver's compartment, is a mechanical fuel pump that drives off the end of the top camshaft. Mechanical rather than electrical fuel pumps are used on Indy cars for two reasons. First, for the sake of simplicity and weight savings, Indy cars do not have full electrical systems. If an electrical fuel pump were to be used, an electrical system would have to be added. Second, a rather large and heavy (by racing standards) electrical motor would be required to supply a thirsty Indy engine with the nearly one-half gallon per mile volume of methanol it requires to propel a car at racing speeds.

A typical view of the wastegate pipe
(top) and exhaust pipes (bottom)
combination exiting a turbocharged
Cosworth powerplant. Note again the
heat shielding around pipes.

A good example of the tight, streamlined cowling around the tail of an Indy racer, as exemplified by this Cosworth-engined 1988 Lola. The upper pipe expels gases from the turbocharger wastegate while the lower pipe expels exhaust gas that has been used to turn the turbocharger impeller. The sponge at the end of the red arrow on the cowl temporarily covers the fresh-air intake for the turbocharger.

COSWORTH
COSWORTH
BRAKE PADS
STP
VALVOLINE
SIMPSON
RACE PRODUCTS
the Wax Shop
DieHard

A good example of the care and effort taken to contain heat within an exhaust system, thereby making the turbocharger more effective and at the same time protecting fiber body panels from blisters and distortion problems. The bundle of exhaust pipes are wrapped in an aluminized blanket and then further isolated from the lower bodywork by an aluminum sheet barrier. The large round opening just aft of the engine is the fresh-air intake from the turbocharger. Keeping heat away from the inlet is another important reason for taking extra insulation efforts.

73

Running gear
Drivetrain, wheels and tires

A Lola transaxle undergoing routine examination, maintenance and gear set changes. Both Lola and March build their chassis around proprietary transaxles with a limited range of engines in mind, primarily the English Cosworth. Transaxles are not readily moved from a Lola to a March chassis and vice versa. Certain engine swaps— for example, the small-block Chevy V-8 with its strong torque characteristics— also are not good candidates to mate with a Lola or March transaxle. Rapid wear or broken internal parts are common problems due to torque loads.

While braking is not an important
aspect of racing at Indianapolis (merely
letting up on the throttle a very small
amount is what drivers strive for),
brakes nevertheless are a component
of major concern and attention. The
high degree of ventilation of this disc
probably better serves to reduce
unsprung weight on the Lola chassis
than it does to dissipate the very
limited amount of heat generated
during actual race conditions at Indy.
Road racing circuits are another story,
of course.

76

A rear tire wheel assembly showing the rotor disc and suspension carrier out in the wheel, and the halfshaft with its inner bearing assembly at the top. In typical race reporting, when it is stated that a halfshaft failed, it normally means this bearing assembly (at top of photo) has failed. The shaft itself seldom breaks and the bearing at the outer end of the hub carrier generally isn't the problem. Heat in particular and manufacturing defects often will be the culprits, and failure of the bearing race or the balls will be the problem.

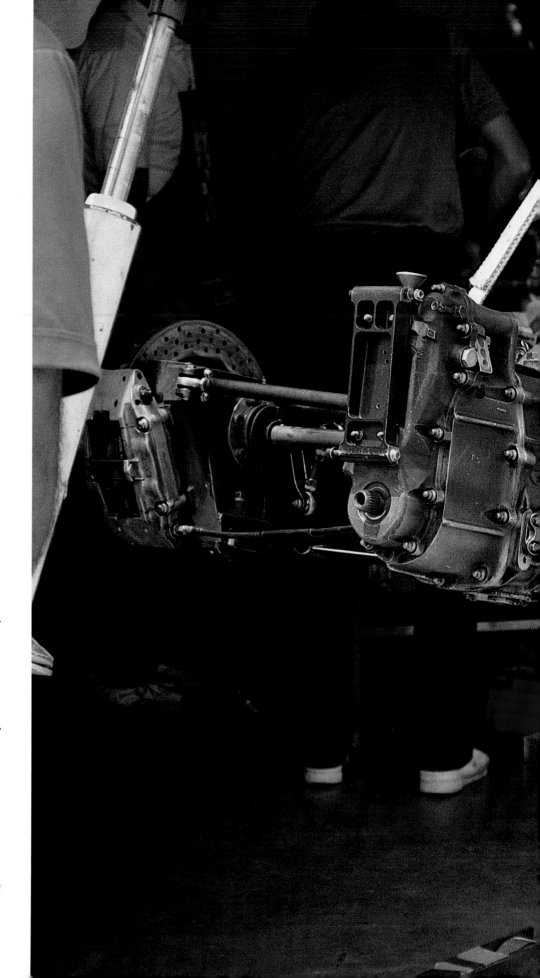

Displaying the obvious modular concept of the modern Indy race car, note here the entire portion of the car aft of the engine, including the turbocharger, transaxle, rear suspension and associated plumbing. These components are removed from the engine as one unit, and are in the process of being mounted on a stand similar to an engine stand. Remember, there is no framework in which the engine sits nor to which the engine and suspension are attached. This assembly of components attaches directly to the engine, which in addition to generating horsepower, must also provide the strength and rigidity to carry suspension loads as well as the weight and forces generated by the transaxle. Note that the brakes here are by Brembo, Italian made and world famous.

Here is an air line connected to a car's pneumatic lift system which is being exercised and tested prior to the car moving out to pit row. The pneumatic lift system is an on-board substitute for the old-fashioned jack found in every vehicle on the highway. When the system is pressurized, pneumatic rams descend from the chassis and lift it off the ground for tire changes or other purposes. It is fast and efficient, and reduces the need for one more piece of equipment in the pit area.

The aft end of a transaxle at the point where the rear wing supports mount. Note the many adjustment holes in the wing supports and how the rear wheel brake lines feed into the lower suspension arms as they travel out to the brake calipers. Of special interest is the aluminum fixture below the wing support attaching point. This is actually the transaxle cooler in a housing designed so that it catches ram air from underneath the car and exhausts it up in the direction of the underside of the rear wing, which is a low-pressure area.

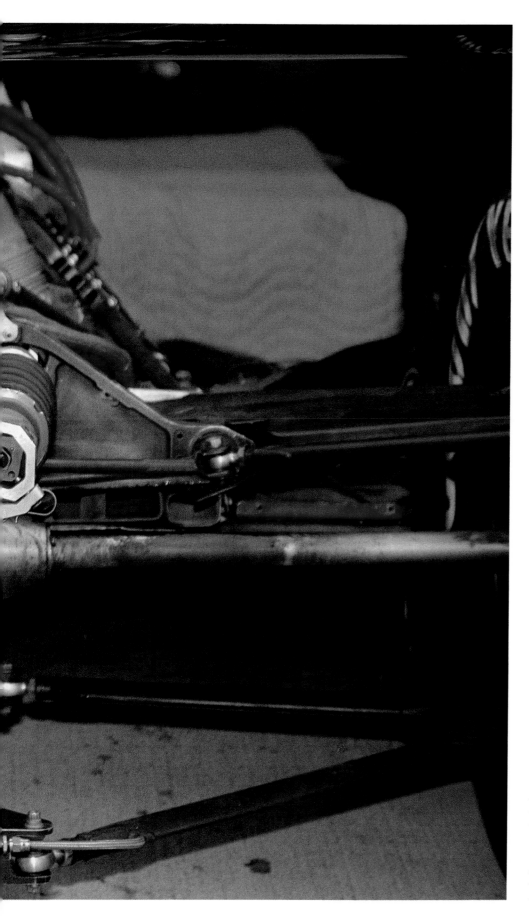

Note again the rear wheel brake lines departing from a common union at the transaxle and traveling through lower suspension arms out the respective wheels. Of particular interest are coil springs and shock absorbers mounted horizontally just to either side of the rear wing upright supports. In order to minimize vertical height requirements and hide as many mechanisms as possible from airflow, designers use a simple and clean system of bell cranks and pivots to transfer rear suspension up-and-down movement to horizontal motion. This allows horizontal placement of shocks and coil-over springs, which allows a more streamlined aerodynamic shape.

83

A close-up of a transaxle on a 1987 Lola showing temperature-sensitive tapes at two points. These tapes change color depending on the temperature to which they are exposed. Note also the safety wiring designated to ensure that fasteners and plugs don't loosen and fall off the unit. The shiny metallic blanket at the top wraps over the top of the transaxle and helps shield the gearbox from exhaust gases, which exit tail pipes directly on top of the transaxle. Generating and reusing more and more heat is at the heart of virtually all attempts to obtain more horsepower from an internal combustion engine of specified formula. Success at this endeavor, though, serves to create added heat dissipation problems.

Approximately 700 to 800 hp must be transmitted by the 7¼ in. clutch on this Chevy Indy V-8 engine. Carbon/carbon clutches are a recent development that offer distinct competitive advantages but as usual, few people in Gasoline Alley wanted to discuss exactly what materials they were using. It seems certain teams used those new ultra-expensive units (prices approach $10,000) but as with anything new, failures as well as successes were being kept very quiet.

As hinted earlier, brake rotors of this nature are of more value and importance on the several road-type courses on which these cars run. At 1,550 pounds of weight and with wide tires, the stopping ability of these cars is phenomenal. A typical Indy car can come to a complete stop in about 500 feet from a speed of 200 mph, and in 300 feet from a speed of 100 mph.

The front suspension of a modern Indy race car, in this case a Lola, is a marvel of cleanliness and simplicity. Typically described as an unequal angle, or asymetrical pushrod suspension, it carries all dampeners, springs and as much linkage as possible inside the chassis and out of the outflow. The total possible movement in an Indy car suspension is approximately only one inch while in comparison the suspension on your family car can travel through a range of six to eight inches.

89

A Goodyear representative with plenty of work ahead of him for a few hours. Like many of the major racing suppliers, Goodyear maintains a full service garage in the Alley during the month of May, providing teams with expert mounting, balancing and problem analysis. Introduction of the radial racing tire at Indy in 1987, with numerous subsequent crashes during practice that year, put special pressures on the Goodyear people to ensure the efficacy of the new design. By 1988, the radial tire was totally integrated into USAC/CART racing—and focus was once again back on horsepower, aerodynamics and suspensions. Tim Parker

Remote rear shock absorber reservoirs glisten in the sun. Finned and positioned to receive a cooling blast of air, these units are attached by braided lines to the actual shock absorber hidden inside the horizontal coil spring just below the red cowling. The blue knob at the forward end of the reservoir can be adjusted to affect the shock's bump setting. The silver fittings at the back of the reservoir allow for air pressurization. Depending on a team's desires and car construction, reservoirs may be positioned so that a driver can make an in-cockpit bump setting adjustment while driving a race.

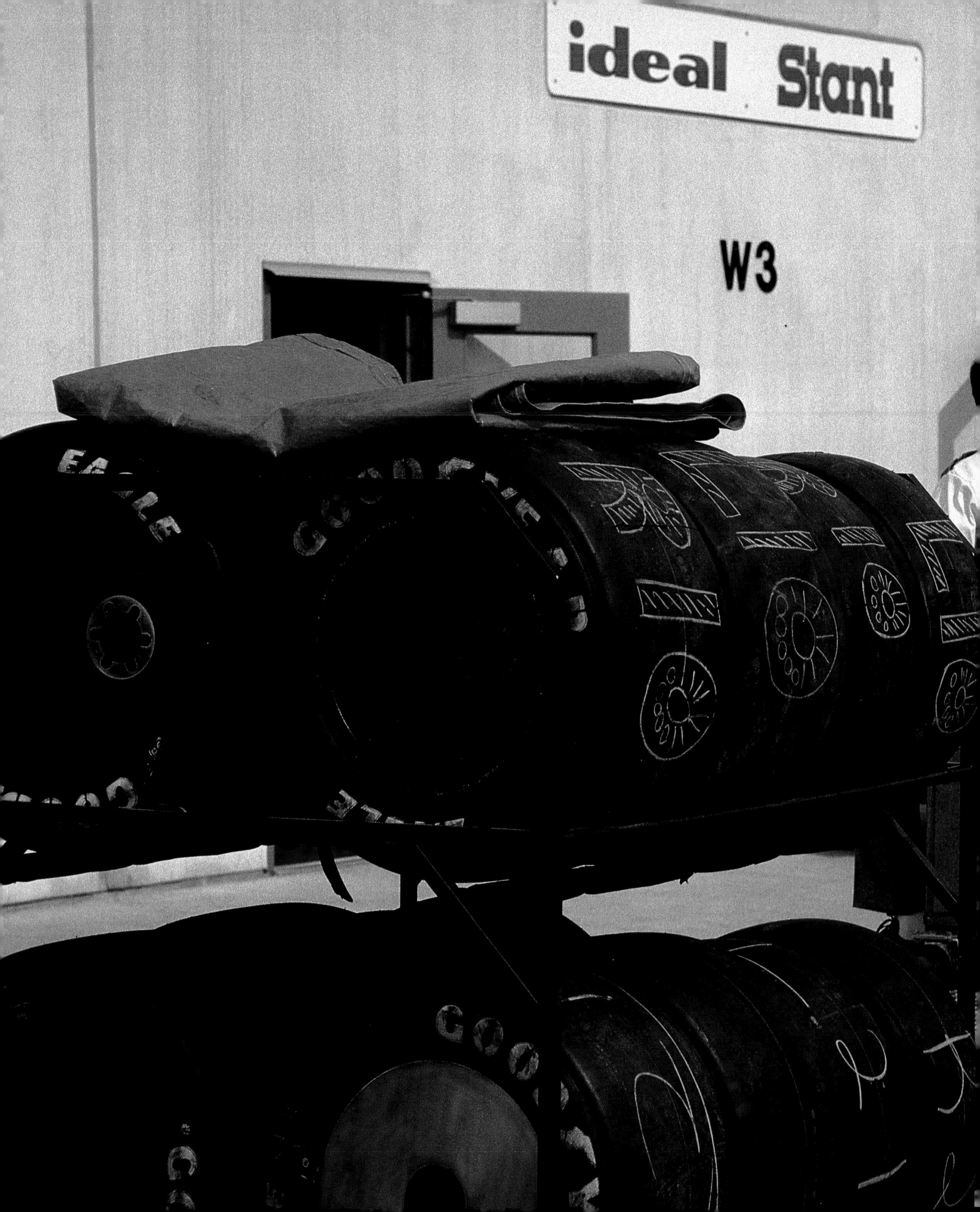

ideal Stant
W3

A well-marked rack of Goodyear tires on the way out to the pits for a practice and qualifying session. This team has gone to considerable lengths to clearly define each tire's various characteristics as well as the location on the car where it will be mounted. Stagger (relating to the exact circumference of each tire and its position on the race car), pressure and compound are three of the more important factors to be considered for each tire. The tarp on the top likely will be used to cover the tires out in the pits to limit the sun's effect. Tire temperatures typically will run in the range of 200 degrees Fahrenheit when an Indy car is at speed, and pressures will be approximately 38 psi in the right front, 36 psi in the right rear and 36 psi in both left side tires. A new tire will carry approximately a ¼ in. thick wear surface, and Goodyear suggests a competitive life of 60 laps for both right side tires, 120 laps for a left front tire and 200 laps for a left rear tire. Goodyear supplies its tire to teams free of cost at Indianapolis, but charges $146 for front tires and $206 for rear tires at all other races.

Bear Automotive, manufacturer of automotive suspension diagnostic and alignment equipment, maintains a facility for examining and adjusting Indy cars during May. Most top-line teams, however, have their own sophisticated portable equipment which they take with them from track to track. At Indianapolis, the typical racer will be set up with toe out on both front wheels, toe in on the right rear wheel and little toe in—maybe even a little toe out—on the left rear wheel. Toe in on the right rear makes that wheel want to turn a left-hand corner. Toe out is set on both front wheels, primarily as a means of getting more cornering power out of the left front tire. As a car enters a left-hand turn at Indy, the driver begins to turn the steering wheel to the left and weight transfers to the right-side tires. The driver continues to turn left until the proper angle is reached by the right front tire, now carrying the majority of the cornering force, so that the car safely turns the corner. With little weight on the left front tire it is seemingly along only for the ride—until you remember that both front wheels are set up with static toe out. By the time the right front wheel has turned far enough to the left to drive the car around the corner, the left front tire will have turned beyond the angle established by the right front and will in fact appear to be turning left at too sharp an angle. This "turned-too-far" condition is tempered, however, by the fact the tire is carrying little weight and thus is not able to generate enough force to cause the car to turn too sharply to the left. It is this turned-too-far condition caused by the initial toe-out setting of both front wheels that allows the left front wheel to generate more turning force than would be the case if both front wheels were set straight ahead. Tim Parker

94

Looking humorous, maybe even a bit like training wheels, is the Domino's Pizza team car mounted on transport wheels and tires. It's not uncommon to see cars in the pits riding on traditional rain tires or rubber of this nature, primarily to provide a bit more ground clearance. Gasoline Alley has definite high and low areas where concrete has been formed to channel away rain water and other fluids. While not pronounced by any standards, these contours will nearly scrape the bottom of the typical Indy racer, which often has only ¾ in. clearance from the ground. Normal rain tires with their thicker tread surface provide just enough added clearance to eliminate scraping.

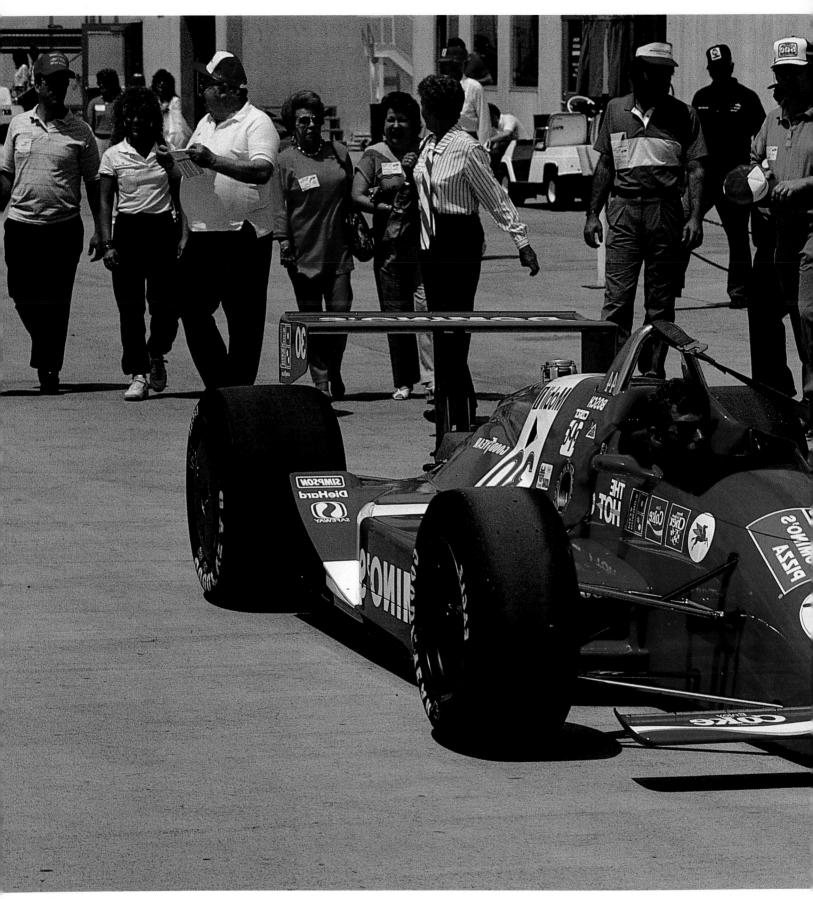

Front and rear wheels are 15 in. in diameter and 10 in. wide. Front tires are 25½ in. in diameter and 10 in. wide. The right rear tire is 27 in. in diameter and 14½ in. wide, while the left rear tire is supplied 14½ in. wide but in three different diameters: 26.82, 26.77 or 26.72 in. These different diameters allow a team some variation in setting up a car's stagger, a term referring to a car's natural tendency, when mounted with tires of differing diameters, to turn right or left. An undersize left rear tire will make an Indy car want to turn to the left, a quality which improves handling, and therefore speed, in each of Indy's four turns per lap.

The cockpit
The driver's office

As ludicrous as it might seem to the uninitiated, steering wheels routinely "come off" race cars. In fact, if they couldn't be detached most drivers could neither get into their cars for a race, nor get out, especially in the event of an accident—a time when a hasty exit is often necessary to escape flames or scalding coolant. The modern Indy car truly fits a driver like the proverbial glove.

This shot is of the cockpit of a 1986 March car. Of particular interest is the red container normally hidden by the driver's seat and mounted in a position approximately under the driver's knees. This is the fire bottle containing retardant for the onboard fire extinguishing system. This particular car was plumbed to empty the bottle's entire contents inside the cockpit. Some teams will run a line to also spray retardant on the engine. Also note the electrical instrument panel containing rows of yellow, green and red lights mounted at the top. This relatively new device produced by Moore Industries, is a tachometer that indicates engine rpm by the illumination of lights. The tachometer can be adjusted to illuminate lights at differing rpm intervals. The green row can be used to indicate rpm shift points and the red indicates excessive rpm. This particular unit is mounted in a stock-block Chevy-engined car with a 7500 rpm shift point. Note the digital 75 figure on the left-hand side, indicating the rpm at which the green lights will illuminate. One of the major benefits of this tachometer is that a driver can monitor rpm with peripheral vision. The conventional tachometer requires a driver to shift attention from the track and concentrate totally on the instrument.

103

A cockpit with all instruments in place, including coolant temperature, oil pressure, tachometer and manifold pressure gauges. The shielded red button activates the fire extinguishing system. The instruments appear to be mounted in a haphazard or crooked manner, at an angle instead of horizontal. Each driver and team have their own thoughts on the subject, but most cars will have the instruments mounted so that when everything is operating properly during a race all needles will point in the same direction. Instruments may be rotated in their mountings so that all needles will point up when indicating normal operation. This allows the driver to spot a problem at a quick glance, which is all the time a driver has to devote to checking his gauges in the heat of a race.

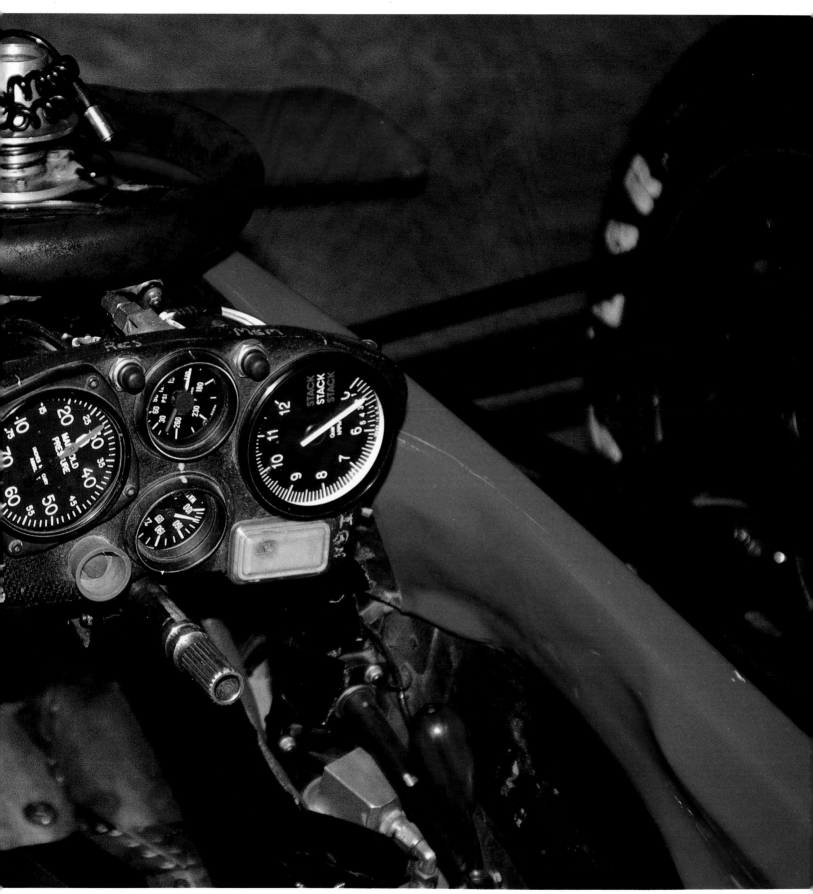

A typical Cosworth engine installation in the 1988 Granatelli Racing Lola. Of special interest are the two lines and the three fittings on top of the intake plenum just aft of the polished pop-off valve. These lines feed the in-cockpit driver boost control and the boost gauge. Drivers are able to alter boost from zero up to 45 inches of mercury by adjusting a control in the cockpit. At 45 in. hg, the pop-off valve begins to open, releasing excess turbo boost pressure. This momentary release of pressure has a significant negative effect on engine performance, often lasting one to two seconds. Thus, tripping a pop-off valve is to be avoided if at all possible. Pop-off valves are required on all cars to ensure a team doesn't exceed the Speedway's maximum allowable turbo boost.

This shot of a cockpit with the windshield and upper cowling removed, provides a look at plumbing and wiring as well as a major front suspension component. As unlikely as it may seem, the stubby transverse-mounted, round object just forward of the panel is the car's front sway bar. The two blades that project forward to links running down to the front suspension can be rotated from the position they are in to one where the flat sides are vertical. This transmits more force to the sway bar (the blades don't flex as much) thus altering the sway bar's spring rate. This adjustment can be made by the driver from inside the cockpit during racing conditions. While a car is set up for optimal handling before a race, changing track conditions, damage and component wear all contribute to a change in handling qualities as a race progresses. Adjusting a car's handling during a race is a valuable advantage but one that must be used judiciously, due to some of the unknowns encountered when an onboard adjustment is made.

With the cockpit just out of the picture to the left, you are looking at three items of importance just behind a driver's head. From left to right is the fuel tank filler neck (this filler is not used during racing pit stops), the funnel-shaped receptacle designed to receive a male pneumatic fitting which extends the pneumatic lifts under the race car, and the much cussed and discussed pop-off valve which limits turbocharger boost according to a preset adjustment.

At speed
What it's all about

What it's all about—Gordon Johncock at speed in the Granatelli Racing 1987 vintage March Cosworth. In spite of this team's financial abilities, an up-to-date chassis and engine combination and a two-time Indy winner at the helm, the car couldn't make the 1988 race. The availability of money is no guarantee of finding the all-too-elusive combination that unlocks a car's full potential.

111

As is the case in Formula One, computer analysis and checkout of various race car functions, especially engine performance, has arrived at the Alley. While not nearly as commonplace as in Formula One, the more sophisticated teams did have a technician and computer equipment. Start-up analysis is usually limited to temperature and oil pressure concerns. On-track measurements are typically made of engine rpm, boost pressure, oil pressure, wheel speed, throttle position and possibly some aerodynamic pressure. This data is typically stored onboard the car and downloaded to a computer after a run is completed.

Everybody has a way of keeping their product's name in front of the spectators. This really great job of turning a fuel tank into a beer can belongs to the Penske team. A typical Indy fuel tank begins life as a standard 350-400 gallon tank manufactured from stainless steel by people such as Kennedy Tank in Indianapolis. A false floor is built into each tank, which cuts total capacity down to approximately 250 gallons. This floor is sloped up at the rear to provide maximum static head pressure at all times. USAC allows a maximum of 243 gallons to be placed in a tank at race time. Each tank must be equipped with manually controlled vent and flow valves which are spring-loaded to close if released. These tanks and their valve mechanisms must receive an annual inspection from USAC prior to approval for pit use.

Previous page

The number 98 Skoal Bandit 1988 Lola
Cosworth on the scales at tech
inspection prior to being released to
the track for practice. Countless factors
are checked during technical
inspection, ranging from the width of
the aerodynamic bodywork to the
quality of safety harness. For the 1988
race, cars with Cosworth and Chevrolet
V-8 (Ilmore Chevrolet) power had to
observe a 1,550 pound minimum
weight limit while the stock-block
Chevy V-8, Buicks and Chevy V-6 could
race with a 1,475 pound minimum
weight. Each car intending to practice
and qualify for the 500 must undergo a
thorough magnaflux test of all metal
components before it is allowed on the
track. If it is involved in an accident,
the car must then have all metal parts
retested before it is again allowed back
on the track.

Designated as the only allowable fuel
for the 500 in 1965, methanol was
selected over gasoline because of its
less explosive and less volatile nature.
Methanol provides more energy per
unit than gasoline, and it burns cooler
in an engine, thus placing less stress on
the typically already overstressed
powerplant. Among its negative
features, though, are the fact that it
corrodes aluminum and it does not
produce a visible flame or smoke when
burning. Thus, pit fires are a real
hazard with methanol because they
can erupt and spread without team
members becoming aware until a
serious situation has developed.

The incomparable A. J. Foyt listens intently as a Cosworth is fired and warmed in one of the five team cars at his disposal. Foyt's 10,612 racing miles at Indy (prior to the 1988 event), his four Indy wins and countless other victories make him a favorite with race fans everywhere. Included in Foyt's stable of cars for the 1988 Indy race was a Chev V-6 stock-block car. This engine was not based on the currently produced small-block Chevrolet V-6 engine but rather on a V-6 version of Chev's big-block V-8 design.

Several teams take a precautionary step to aid the warm-up of a cold engine and help ensure proper lubrication by using a heating probe. This device, shown here emerging from just behind the rollover bar and connected by an electrical line, is simply a rheostatically controlled heating dipstick which sits in the oil tank and warms the lubricant to a desired temperature. The normally used 50-weight oil is thinned somewhat by this heating, thus is more readily pumped through the engine during the critical first seconds when an engine comes to life. Teams using synthetic oils don't appear to be as concerned about cold start lubrication.

INDY TENTS

INDIANAPOLIS RENTAL TENTS

1988 USAC

CHAMPION

COSWORTH

The Granatelli team's car is fired up for a practice lap. It's interesting to note that much of the last-minute starting-line drama of 20 years ago, when the inevitable one or two engines couldn't be started for the race, was due not to engine problems but to problems associated with these units. Earlier starter motors typically turned the old Offenhauser at only 400 rpm—barely enough to fire the engine. If a crew wasn't careful, it would end up with a badly flooded engine and precious little time to correct the problem.

123

Previous page
Mobile trackside command posts accompany teams at the major USAC and CART races such as Indy. Electronic timers, calculators, race car communication equipment, display tubes, radio links to timing and scoring, plus spare components comprise these rolling nerve centers.

A 1988 Lola Cosworth at speed departing turn four and entering the front straightaway. Tire construction, ground effects and wing development all have had major impacts on performance of race cars in corners. Ten years ago the difference in cornering speed versus straightaway speeds was in the range of 25 mph. With recent developments, the differential has dropped to about 8 mph, causing a sharp increase in overall top speeds in spite of more restrictive engine limitations.

Perhaps one of the most widely recognized symbols of the 500, the scoring pylon serves the dual purposes of displaying qualification positions for each car during the two weekends prior to the race and the running position of each car during the race. It is this pylon and several lighted signs located around the track that are the primary means by which on-site spectators keep abreast of the ever-changing situations on the track. Once the race has run 10 to 20 laps, the whole event becomes a blur of colors and sounds with the average viewer unable to see more than a limited length of the track and unable to keep current on the positions of respective cars.